msme

8455694981

Gieri Iorlano

A South American hoatzin

CLOSE-UP
A Focus on Nature

SILVER BURDETT PRESS

© 1995 Silver Burdett Press
Published by Silver Burdett Press.
A Simon & Schuster Company
299 Jefferson Road, Parsippany, NJ 07054
Printed in the United States of America
10 9 8 7 6 5 4 3 2 1

Library of Congress
Cataloging-in-Publication Data
Hamilton, Jean (Barbara Jean)
   Tropical rainforests/by Jean Hamilton; photographs
by Frank Balthis . . . [et al.].
      p. cm.--(Close up)
   Originally published: San Luis Obispo, Calif.: Blake
Pub., 1993.
   ISBN 0-382-24868-6 (LSB)
   ISBN 0-382-24869-4 (SC)
   1. Rain forest ecology--Juvenile literature. 2. Rain
forests--Juvenile literature. [1. Rain forests. 2. Rain forest
ecology. 3. Ecology.] I. Balthis, Frank, ill. II. Title.
III. Title: Tropical rain forests. IV. Series: Close up
(Parsippany, N.J.)
[QH541.5.R27H35 1994]   94-31821
574.5'2642'0913--dc20   CIP
                                               AC

Tropical RAINFORESTS

Writer
Jean Hamilton

Series Editor
Vicki León

Photographers
Frank Balthis, Hans and Judy Beste,
John Cancalosi, John Chellman, E.R. Degginger,
Michael Fogden, Francois Gohier, Martha Hill, Steven Holt,
Breck P. Kent, Frans Lanting, Richard K. LaVal, Wayne Lynch,
Kevin Schafer, Dr. Nigel Smith, Larry Ulrich,
Doug Wechsler, Belinda Wright

Designer
Ashala Nicols Lawler

SILVER BURDETT PRESS

© 1995 Silver Burdett Press
Published by Silver Burdett Press.
A Simon & Schuster Company
299 Jefferson Road,
Parsippany, NJ 07054
Printed in the United States of America
10 9 8 7 6 5 4 3 2 1

An Eden worth saving

THIS IS THE FOREST PRIMEVAL, the emerald mansion that enchants and frightens us, green and glistening as a wet leaf, largely unexplored yet vanishing before our eyes like mist off the trees after a tropical rainstorm. Forty-five million years ago, the world was a paradise of tropical rainforests almost pole to pole. We've found fossil pollen from rainforest species in such widely separated and unlikely places as London, Alaska, and Tennessee. With the coming of the first Ice Age, the rainforest retreated to the latitudes near the equator.

In the last two million years, the green belt around the earth's middle has alternately shrunk and expanded as the Ice Ages have come and gone. For millennia now, the rainforest has stretched almost unbroken across the land surfaces on either side of the equator, extending north to the Tropic of Cancer and south to the Tropic of Capricorn. Today, however, satellite photographs show the belt in tatters, its heartland burnt and cut into blocks and patches.

This time, the villain in Eden isn't the snake. Human pressures are putting tropical paradise in jeopardy. Acre for acre, this moist, mysterious ecosystem has more variety than a hundred supermarket shelves. Researchers have counted 125 different mammals, 150 species of butterflies, 400 species of birds, and 750 distinct kinds of trees in a typical patch four miles square.

Over half of what remains is found in Latin America, most of that in the Amazon and Orinoco basins of Brazil and Venezuela. Another 25% survives in the Asian tropics, and about 20% in Central and West Africa, with scattered stands in Australia, India, and some Caribbean and Pacific Islands. Today's rainforest covers just 7% of the earth's land surface, yet still contains at least half of the world's estimated five million species of living things.

ALL TRUE RAINFORESTS SHARE CERTAIN QUALITIES: tropical heat and heavy rainfall distributed evenly throughout the year, certain types of vegetation, and species of great diversity and interdependence. The temperature averages 80°F, with more fluctuation between day and night than from month to month. A true equatorial forest receives between 160 and 400 inches of rain each year. This warm, wet, stable environment creates and nourishes untold biological riches.

Five main groups of vegetation can be found in all rainforests. Most noticeable are the free-standing plants that photosynthesize: shrubs, herbs, and great trees, standing like cathedral columns, often buttressed by huge slabs.

Members of the next three groups – climbers, stranglers, and epiphytes or air plants – also contain chlorophyll and make their own food, but need supports to grow on. The most familiar climbers

are the long liana vines of Tarzan fame. In reality, lianas do not provide very reliable transportation unless you're a monkey making a short hop. Climbers get their start when sunlight floods through a gap in the forest roof. Rooted in the soil, they use trees as trellises as they cling and twist their way to the canopy. There they form a network of woody loops and links, an aerial highway for the creatures that live in the upper stories.

Like climbers, stranglers twine around for support, in the process often killing their host tree. The most common stranglers belong to the genus *Ficus*. The strangler fig leads a double life, beginning as an air plant germinated in the crotch of a branch from a seed dropped by a passing bird or fruit bat. Aerial roots creep to the forest floor, dig in, establish a firm hold, then climb back toward the sunlight. In time,

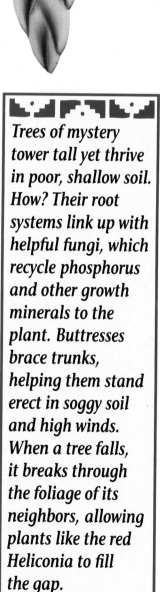

Trees of mystery tower tall yet thrive in poor, shallow soil. How? Their root systems link up with helpful fungi, which recycle phosphorus and other growth minerals to the plant. Buttresses brace trunks, helping them stand erect in soggy soil and high winds. When a tree falls, it breaks through the foliage of its neighbors, allowing plants like the red Heliconia to fill the gap.

the roots meld together to form a living coffin around the host tree. The now-dead interior of the host becomes a home to a variety of animals. When a rainforest is cleared by humans for lumber or cattle pasture, often the tough, opportunistic strangler is the only source of food and shelter to survive.

EPIPHYTES MAKE THEIR HOMES ON bark and branches. Unlike stranglers, they are harmless tenants. Many are ferns, mosses, and other non-flowering plants. The showiest ones let us know we are truly in a rainforest: the orchids and bromeliads. These botanical hitchhikers thrive on a diet of sunlight and moisture; many have deep cuplike interiors that form waterholes and habitat for other canopy dwellers.

The last group includes plants without chlorophyll: parasites like tropical mistletoe that dig their roots deep into a tree's circulatory system, and saprophytes, the molds and fungi that feed on rotting material and form the cleanup crew of the forest floor.

In other kinds of forests, you can walk for miles and see the same stands of hardwoods or evergreens. But a typical acre-patch of rainforest contains as many as 60 different species of trees. Why this riotous variety? First, the great age of this ecosystem. Second, the constancy of the environment. With no droughts or cold snaps to send seeds into hiding or produce rigid mating seasons, reproduction is an ongoing celebration. Some scientists argue that while these factors could maintain large numbers of species, they could not produce them. Others favor the "refuge theory" proposed in 1969 by German ornithologist Jurgen Haffer. Noticing the

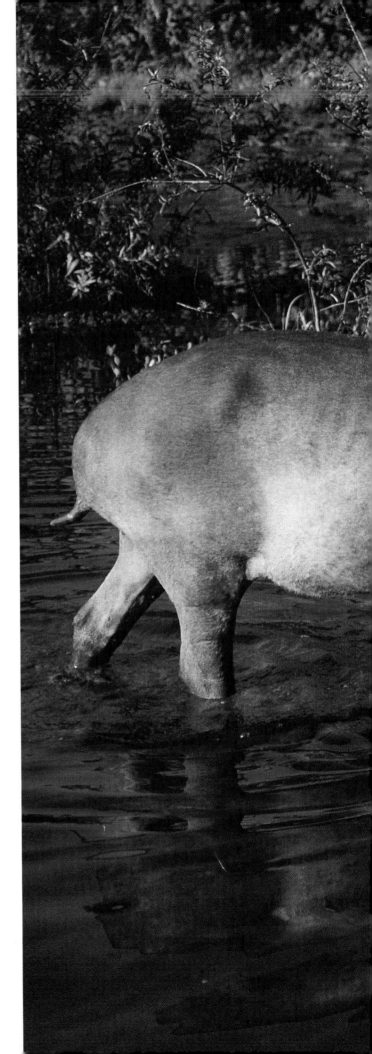

Floor grazing mammals in Mexican, South American, and Southeast Asian rainforests include the tapir. An elusive plant eater related to the rhino and the horse, the tapir also browses along riverbanks. In the African rainforest, the forest hog fills a similar niche.

large number of bird species found in one place in the Amazon, he suggested that the cold, dry periods of the Ice Ages may have split large areas of rainforest into small "forest islands" where favorable conditions still existed.

magine a bird population, all of the same species. As a glacier makes its way from the north, the climate changes, the habitat becomes unsuitable. Half the population retreats to Refuge A, half to Refuge B. Each group changes over time in response to its local environment. When the glacier retreats, the two populations rejoin. Because of the changes each has undergone, interbreeding may no longer be possible. Where there was one species, now there are two. It's possible that the stable-appearing rainforest owes much of its mosaic character to this sort of disturbance and change.

The architecture of the rainforest creates vertical as well as horizontal niches. Trees commonly grow to 20-story skyscraper heights, making mini- and micro-habitats at different levels. Because of its great height, the rainforest uses solar energy more efficiently than any other ecosystem. Compare it to a cornfield, where solar energy isn't turned into biological energy until it reaches the corn at eight or nine feet. In the rainforest, the vegetation absorbs the sun's energy at the top of the pavilion, again in the canopy, and in lower levels as it filters down.

Finally, the rainforest is remarkable in its interdependence. Examples are everywhere. For instance, each species of fig tree is pollinated by its own species of wasp. The wasp in return receives a site to lay its eggs. The Brazil nut tree is pollinated by one type of bee, but the germination of its seed requires the services of an agouti, a South American rodent that chews and softens the seed coat. In a field study, just one bromeliad plant was found to contain: four daddy-long-legs, a brown spider brooding eggs, a jumping millipede, a scorpion, three kinds of woodlice, numerous small beetles, earwigs, a tree seedling, a cockroach, aquatic fly larvae, a small brown frog, and an earthworm with a brilliant blue nose. All paid for their lodging with their waste products, supplying the plant with nutrients. Each element of the rainforest raises the life expectancy of another element, and ultimately of the rainforest itself.

Of the remaining rainforests, the Amazonian is by far the largest and richest. It covers 2.5 million square miles – almost 40% of South America. One-third of the world's flowering plants, more than half of the world's bird species, and so many fish and insects only a fraction have been identified, call it home. Like other rainforests, it can be divided into four levels: the floor, understory, canopy, and the emergent layer or pavilion.

The floor

Whether in Latin America, Asia, the Pacific Islands, or Africa, the floor looks much the same. Unlike the jungles pictured in films or books, it's not an impenetrable wall of green. Skyward, you see tree trunks disappearing into a solid layer of foliage, but the floor is quite open and passable. Plants here adapt to a life of shade and deprivation. Ferns, small shrubs, molds, fungi, and saplings wait for light from a gap in the canopy so they can begin an upward journey that may take a hundred years. The soil is old and impoverished. Because of the high humidity, decay is rapid, and the shallow roots of living vegetation take up nutrients quickly. Leaf litter breaks down in six weeks, compared with one year in a deciduous forest. As a result, there is nothing left to feed the soil itself.

Animal waste that might go back to fertilize the earth in a temperate forest is quickly claimed by insects, especially beetles. Male beetles of the *Canthon* species slice off pieces of dung with their hind legs. A female selects her mate by the size of his dung ball, which she scrambles onto as the male rolls it a few yards away. They mate, depositing the eggs on the dung ball, sometimes sharing a nuptial feast before they bury the prize which later feeds their brood.

Insects are everywhere: beetles, mantids, flies, butterflies, bees, grasshoppers, wasps, mosquitoes, and more. Most numerous of all are termites and ants.

Although they often prefer to live high in the matapalos or strangler fig, anoles and other lizards use the floor as a battleground. They display to other males by expanding their dewlaps, sometimes drawing the attention of lizard-loving birds in the bargain.

The most spectacular termite nests begin on a subterranean level, like parking garages, often rising into mounds up to seven feet high. A single acre of forest may hold a thousand termitaries, each jammed with as many as ten million termites. One million of these tireless insects can consume 12 tons of dead wood in a year. Without them, the rainforest would soon disappear under its own litter.

A termitary begins with the flight of thousands of winged termites, potential kings and queens 20 times larger than the workers. A "princess" drops to the ground, discards her hinged wings, and signals to any male who has survived the flight that she's ready to set up housekeeping. (Few royal couples live to reproduce because the act of swarming attracts so many hungry predators.) The new couple digs down into moist soil to prepare their "gardens," fertilizing them with partially digested wood and irrigating them with moisture from their own bodies. When a white mold appears in the gardens, the queen lays her eggs and rears workers to run the colony. This accomplished, she retires to a cell with her consort and continues to lay eggs, perhaps 5,000 a day for the next 15 years or so. Eventually she becomes so obese that she can no longer leave her chamber, but the still-svelte king remains with her. When she stops laying eggs, the workers depose the queen by sucking her dry, leaving an empty husk. This in turn sets off the next nuptial flight.

RAINFOREST ANT POPULATIONS EASILY OUTWEIGH and outnumber all the vertebrates in a given area. Colonies of *Atta* or leaf-cutter ants may contain millions of workers, each specializing as a guard, forager, or soldier. In 1984, biologists discovered a curious way in which ants seem to control their numbers. As they enter or leave the nest, soldier ants stroke the antennae of the other workers. At the beginning of the rainforest "dry season," the smaller workers respond to the greeting by attacking and dismembering the larger soldiers. Although their sickle-shaped mandibles could easily defeat the workers, the soldiers offer no resistance. Human researchers concluded that the colony was pruning itself of larger mouths to feed in the lean times ahead.

Army ants, closely related to the legendary driver ants of Africa, set up temporary camps each night. Soldiers link themselves together to form a nest where nurses tend the queen and larvae. At dawn, the soldiers stream out and attack everything in their path, tearing it to pieces and carrying it back to camp. At dusk, the army moves to a new site. For the next two weeks, this raiding and camping continues. When the larvae begin to spin cocoons, the colony settles down for about three weeks. The queen then lays as many as 300,000 eggs which hatch into new larvae. Meanwhile, new workers emerge from the cocoons and in a couple of days, the colony is off again to repeat the cycle. Nothing can stop them except fire and wide rivers. They easily cross streams by hooking their legs to form a living bridge or raft.

But what of the other creatures of the rainforest floor? Many rely on camouflage to stay hidden. Other are small or live nocturnal lives. It takes patience and an eye for detail to find them. A stump may turn out to be a brown bird or an agouti. A vine may be an emerald tree boa or an iguana's tail. A twig becomes a walking-stick; a pile of dry leaves,

A shy insectivore, the anteater rarely gets involved in confrontations with anything larger than an ant. When it does, it assumes a defensive posture, as this collared anteater of Costa Rica has. It most often uses its heavy claws to break into nests so it can vacuum up the insects it finds there. Adept at climbing trees, some anteaters have prehensile or grasping tails to help them handle the ups and downs of daily life.

a coiled fer-de-lance; a rock, an armadillo rolled into a ball; and the bark of a tree takes flight as an iridescent blue morpho butterfly.

There are extroverted exceptions. In a clearing, you might come upon several dozen male cocks-of-the-rock, where they pose and parade for eligible females in a courtship area called a lek. The males advertise boldly with bright golden plumage and legs, beak, eyes, and skin of brilliant orange. The brown and dowdy hens select a male, quickly mate, then retire to build a nest and lay eggs. The cocks continue their display as long as hens appear on the scene. At first glance it may appear that the male has the best of it, idling about in nature's tropical singles' bar, while the female raises the young alone. One study showed, however, that over half the males failed to attract a female. In a Darwinian sense, they are the losers, forever preening and posturing but never passing on their genes.

THE BEST PLACE TO SEE RAINFOREST floor animals is at the edge of the river. There lurks the giant anaconda, largest of the world's snakes, waiting for the unwary to come and drink. The capybara, largest of all rodents, feeds on plants in the river and along the shore. The hoatzin, a chicken-sized bird of ancient lineage, builds its nest in trees along the bank. If alarmed, the fledglings drop into the water and swim into the tangled vegetation. The young have two movable claws near the tip of each wing, useful for clambering back into the nest. Even after the claws are lost at maturity, the birds continue to use their wings like hands. Baby hoatzins bear an uncanny resemblance to the *Archaeopteryx*, the earliest known bird, which came on the scene about 100 million years ago.

Amid the great trees of the rainforest, tiny creatures predominate. An important recycler, the dung beetle (above left) wins a mate and tidies the floor at the same time. Structures built by tireless termites are a common sight. Deforestation of the rainforests has vastly increased termite numbers. A recent survey estimates there are 310 pounds of termites for each of the 5+ billion people on earth. In contrast to life forms that use concealment as a strategy, gaudy cocks-of-the-rock openly strut their stuff on the forest floor.

A rainforest may have more ants – in weight and in sheer numbers – than anything else. Leaf-cutter or Atta ant colonies can number over five million individuals. Army ants, famous and feared, follow scent trails along the floor to hunt down sources of food. The ant at right is a worker, the ant at left, a soldier. Native doctors use the soldier's oversized jaws or mandibles as sutures for wounds.

Jaguars, the largest predators in the Amazonian rainforest, prey on pig-like peccaries and tapirs, pursuing them into the river for a sunset kill. Many river creatures are equally at home on land, including crocodiles, an odd turtle called the matamata, the yapok, the only aquatic marsupial, and leeches waiting to hitch a warm-blooded ride. Strangest of all is the lungfish, which can gulp air in the manner of its ancestors that adapted to stagnant lakes some 350 million years ago.

Another curious animal dwelling on the rainforest floor is the giant anteater. With huge curved claws it makes short work of a termite nest, then captures the insects on its sticky 24-inch tongue.

Clearly the rainforest floor teems with life, but the forest gives up its secrets reluctantly. Chances are your first impression would be of a humid, eerie silence, broken only by the hum and drone of insects and permeated with the sweet, musky smells of growth and decay.

Frogs do it en massse. Sing, that is. Scientists have discovered that male frogs form choruses not to outcroak one another but for safety in numbers. Many rainforest amphibians are bright and shiny as jellybeans, such as this red-eyed leaf frog. Sticky pads on frog fingers and toes let them move easily in any direction on leaf and tree surfaces.

The biggest meat-eaters often live in the under-story. These margeys, thought to hunt at night, live in the same habitat as ocelets, which are day predators. Although they all live in Latin American rainforests, margeys and ocelets are much smaller than the jaguar, a hunter of deer and tapir. In Asia, the tiger ranks as the top rainforest predator. In Africa, it's the leopard.

The understory

THE NEXT LEVEL, CALLED THE understory, rises from the ground to about 60 feet. Because so little of the sunlight filters through the canopy to this level, the air itself appears tinged with green. As on the floor, the humidity is high and the temperature constant. Leaves are oblong with a pointed "drip-tip" that lets rain drain off quickly. Why? Because dry leaves are safer from attack by fungi than wet ones. Here we find flowers and fruit that grow directly out of the tree trunks rather than from the branches, an energy saver when sunlight is at a premium. More than a thousand species exhibit this adaptation, called cauliflory. They are found almost exclusively at this level. Cacao, our source for chocolate, is one.

Understory plants rely heavily on fruit bats to carry their seeds to new locations. If the seeds simply drop to the foot of the parent tree, overcrowding will result. In a botanical sense, the fleshy part of a fruit is just window-dressing, a way of making the seed attractive to the animals that pick it, eat it, and carry it away in their digestive tracts for dispersal. Originally, all New World bats ate insects. Over time, they have filled many feeding niches afforded by the richness of the tropics. Now they are specialists that eat fruit, insects, nectar, pollen, fish, lizards, mice, birds, frogs, or even other bats. Despite their bad press, vampire bats rarely attack humans. Only one

of three species feeds on mammalian blood, usually that of cattle and hogs.

The animals best suited for the tightly-knit runways of the understory tend to be small and lightweight. Tails are often long, bushy, and used for counterbalance. Hands and feet are adapted for grasping, like those of the coati, a raccoon relative. Traveling in bands of up to 40, coatis are opportunists, feeding on whatever they can catch, including frogs.

NO ANIMAL IS MORE PERFECTLY designed for life in the understory than the tree frog. Each frog finger or toe comes with a suction cup that secretes a sticky mucus, letting them climb the sheerest of vertical surfaces. Here, too, we find geckos and chameleons with oddly shaped feet. A chameleon clamps two toes on one side of a limb and three on the other, making for a sturdy grip. Tree-dwelling reptiles and amphibians often give birth to live young rather than laying eggs as their ground-dwelling counterparts do. The tree species have fewer offspring, but the young have more opportunity for survival because of the time they spend in the mother's body. Provided, of course, their mother doesn't become a meal for a coati.

The understory is also home to the ocelot and the margey. Rare after decades of being hunted for the fur trade, these small, elegant cats have coats that blend with dappled light.

The canopy

MOVING INTO THE CANOPY, located from 60 to 120 feet above the ground, the climate changes: more air movement, more temperature variation, and less humidity. From an airplane, the canopy looks like vast, tidy fields of broccoli. From below, it appears as a maze of twisted, interlocking branches, vines, and streamer-like lianas. Both views are misleading. To the creatures that live in it, the canopy is a sunlit paradise with room to fly, glide, or leap about. Toucans, hawks, owls, pigeons, hummingbirds, and a vivid array of parrots and macaws make their home here.

Parrots climb about the canopy with ease, foraging for a variety of seeds, fruits, and flowers. Not only do they feed in the treetops, they bathe, socialize, and nest here. Sought after as pets for their beauty and intelligence, these birds are rapidly losing habitat to deforestation. Several of the macaws and many of the Amazon parrot species are already on CITE's critically endangered list.

With their boat-shaped bills, toucans can reach the most distant branches for fruits and berries. Almost as long as the bird's body and distinctively colored in each species, the bill is more than a feeding tool. In a forest full of toucans, it helps each species spot its own kind and find a mate. South American toucans resemble the hornbills of Africa. Both families have huge, bright bills and slender bodies; both nest in tree cavities and include fruit in their diets. They are not, however, closely related, and represent an instance

Only recently have biologists been able to study the secrets of the canopy at first hand. In this airy region, alive with the calls of birds, monkeys, and insects, rainforest orchids and other flowers bloom. Among the loveliest are the epiphytes or air plants such as this bromeliad, whose water-filled centers often support little worlds of plants and animals.

of convergent evolution, where body shape and behavior are a response to similar environmental demands.

Canopy monkeys show how similar animals can coexist peacefully by occupying different levels. The howler monkey lives mostly in the upper reaches and has a sweet tooth for figs, plums, and cacao beans. The spider monkey favors the middle layers and prefers wild nutmeg and bean-like nuts. Capuchins live in the lower part of the canopy, sometimes descending to the understory and floor. The douroucouli also forages from the canopy to the floor, but is active at night. Most other primates are day feeders.

Each species claims territory by calling; especially infamous is the howler, whose vocal displays are said to be among the loudest produced by any animal. In dense foliage, calling is a good way to maintain contact. By howling or chattering, troop members advise each other of their whereabouts, warn of danger, and pinpoint food and water sources.

The spider monkey lays claim to being the most talented acrobat of the canopy, with long limbs, slender body, and an extremely talented tail. Along with a few other South American species, the spider monkey has a prehensile or grasping tail, used as an extra hand. Monkeys are not the only canopy residents equipped with such tails. The raccoon-like kinkajou, the prehensile-tailed porcupine, and two kinds of arboreal anteaters, the silky and the tamandua, also roam the treetops with extra tail-end assurance.

Lemurs, a group of rainforest prosimians now confined to the island of Madagascar, also spiral through the canopy in dazzling gymnastics. Their long, busy tails serve more for balance than for grasping, however. Another aid to arboreal agility among primates is a hand-over-hand way of traveling called brachiation. The gibbons and orangutans of Asia, and the chimpanzees and gorillas of Africa are brachiators, using their hands as hooks rather than graspers.

Sharp eyes are needed to spot two-toed and three-toed sloths, hidden among the leaves by algae which give a greenish hue to their shaggy fur. Algae are not the only freeloaders on the sloth. One individual can harbor many different species of insects. A sloth lives its whole life hanging upside down from a tree branch by its long curved claws. There it eats, breeds, raises young, and mainly sleeps, remaining motionless for up to 18 hours at a time. In the rainforest, slowness has its rewards. The sloth has a metabolic rate about half that of mammals its own size, so it needs less energy to maintain itself in its hot, humid, canopy home.

The pavilion

AS THE TALLER TREES EMERGE from the canopy, their leafy peaks, 120 to 150 feet high, form the pavilion. This is the borderland between forest and sky – a place of strong winds, torrential showers, and burning tropical sun. It can also be a place of great beauty.

As in the other levels, insects densely populate the pavilion. There are hordes of mosquitoes, including those that carry malaria and yellow fever. When a rainforest is cut, they come down with it to prey upon humans and lower-story animals. Swifts, whippoorwills, nighthawks, and other birds that capture insects on the wing find the pavilion a prime feeding area. The New World turkey vulture floats on updrafts above the tree crowns, using its uncanny sense of smell to detect carrion or dead meat far below. Contrary to popular belief, vultures do not prefer rotten meat, so the search for food is a race against time and other scavengers. Once a meal is sniffed out, the vulture lands in the canopy and slowly hops its way to the floor. Other turkey vultures may join in the feast but the squabbling so typical of a flock of African vultures is absent. The South American variety dines slowly, even decorously, until forced to give way to the king vulture. Because its own sense of smell is poor, the king vulture lets its relative lead it to a carcass. Here, too, interdependence is at work. With its stronger beak, the king vulture

Few humans get a chance to see and smell the rainforest in bloom. At unpredictable intervals, the great trees explode with color. In 24 hours or less, the crowns may turn solid pink, yellow, or cream, then shower the ground with waves of flowers, a perfumed feast for the creatures below. Insects and birds are about all that can tolerate the climate extremes of the pavilion trees. At left, the protective mimicry of a katydid doesn't always work when a hunting spider gets hungry. And a spiny katydid uses armor to make itself into a sharp mouthful.

can tear open tough skin that the smaller birds cannot manage. When the king has finished, the turkey vultures return to feed.

The top predator of the pavilion is the largest and most powerful of the eagles, the harpy. Typically larger than the male, the female harpy has feet the size of a man's, tipped with lethally sharp talons. The wings are short and rounded, an adaptation for flying through trees rather than above them. A harpy can chase a hapless monkey through the canopy at a speed of 50 miles per hour. The male and female build huge, messy nests, and together raise the young. Although two eggs are laid, once the first chick hatches, the second is ignored. If it does hatch, it is usually pecked to death by the first. The second egg seems to act as genetic insurance. Other species use this tactic also.

Few reptiles and amphibians brave the heights of the pavilion. As cold-blooded animals, they prefer the moisture and constancy of lower levels. One exception is the flying gecko. It doesn't fly, of course, but makes spectacular glides by means of webbed toes and flaps of skin along its legs, sides, and tail. The flaps open like a parachute as the animal soars from tree to tree.

In every level of the rainforest, animals survive in the places where they can make the best living for themselves. No matter how strange an adaptation appears at first glance, it seems just right when we look closely at its owner's ecological address.

When Bates, Wallace, Humboldt, and other 19th-century naturalists came to the rainforest, they had to content themselves with exploring the floor, and with tales told by local tribespeople. Attempts to study the upper stories were largely unsuccessful. Monkeys were trained to retrieve items from high in the canopy, but too often the monkeys ate the specimens. Trees were felled in the name of science but most of the objects of investigation did not survive the fall. Birds and mammals were shot and sent to museums for taxonomic purposes, but little was learned of their behavior or relationships with other species.

In 1929, British explorer Major R.W.G. Hingston built a platform in a Guiana forest

From the rosy periwinkle, a flower now in danger of vanishing from the Madagascar rainforest, comes the most effective drug we have yet found against children's leukemia. It's just one of the many potent weapons against disease that the rainforest offers. How many more still await discovery?

from which he and his colleagues made their observations. Other platforms, towers, and even an 8-story ladder were constructed by the researchers who followed Hingston. These early efforts allowed scientists to see only those creatures in the immediate vicinity. In 1970, a platform with hundreds of yards of connecting catwalks was designed by U.S. Army engineers in West Malaysia. These platforms extended the areas of study but altered the natural environment, affecting the behavior and growth patterns of canopy residents. Nine years later, in Costa Rica, American biologist Donald Perry developed an aerial network of ropes which gives access to about an acre of rainforest, from ground level to the pavilion. Today's arboreal naturalists conduct long-term studies equipped with an array of inflatable rafts, slings, harnesses, pulleys, mechanical ascenders, and other gear that would astound the first adventurers.

SOON THERE MAY NOT BE MUCH rainforest to study, pristine or otherwise. It is estimated that a hundred acres of rainforest is laid waste each minute, most of it cleared for timber, cattle pasture, and "slash and burn" farming. Each year, an area roughly the size of Newfoundland disappears. Biologists say that unlike other ecosystems, a destroyed rainforest is gone forever, taking with it untold species of animals and plants.

We are beginning to recognize the enormity of such a loss, and how it would affect the earth and its people. The rainforest provides a wealth of vital food, medicines, and products for humankind. Even more disturbing is the effect the destruction of the rainforest could be having on global climate. When rainforests are burned, carbon dioxide is released in massive quantities into the atmosphere. These materials may be second only to the combustion engine in fostering the greenhouse effect.

But all is not gloom and doom. There are many people working on ways to save the rainforest even as it threatens to vanish.

For example, the Smithsonian Tropical Research Institute funds three projects that could provide practical alternatives to deforestation. Two involve the domestication of forest animals as substitutes for beef. One is the paca, reportedly as tasty as suckling pig, which can be raised on tropical fruit. The other is the iguana, a six-foot lizard that tastes like chicken. Both animals can be raised with little impact on the natural environment, producing a cash crop for local farmers. The third project explores the cultivation of selected plants in worn-out cattle pasture. *Acacia manguim*, a tree belonging to the legume family, is capable of drawing nutrients from deep soil and rocks. Not only does it grow to 100 feet in just three years, but it feeds and revitalizes the soil as it grows. The result? Fast-growing trees for timber, and the restoration of the soil for the cultivation of other crops.

These discoveries show that it's possible to use the forest and conserve it at the same time. This is not a new ethic – just one we've forgotten or ignored. For centuries, the tribal peoples who live in and around the rainforests of the world have harvested such products as fruit, nuts, medicines, and rubber without damaging the trees or destroying the ecosystem. Now, over half of the world's original rainforest is gone. At the current rate of destruction, another quarter is expected to disappear by the year 2000. Why should we worry about this magnificent but distant habitat, thousands of miles from most of our own backyards? Because the rainforest is the ancient home of fellow human beings. Because we are threatened with the loss of countless species of plants and animals. Because the forest is a source of new foods, drugs, raw materials – even energy. On a more urgent note, because the same ozone layer covers and protects us all and keeps our planet healthy. The rainforest *is* our own backyard.

In the nick of time, the world is coming to realize that the rainforest is worth more alive than dead: rubber, coffee, oils, spices, medicines, fruits, nuts – even iguanas can be harvested without harming the forest.

WHO LIVES ON LEAVES?

MANY RAINFOREST DENIZENS: birds like the blue-faced hoatzin on the first page. Lizards like the iguana. Mammals from the sloth (page 29) to the high-decibel howler monkey at left.

As a diet, leaves have many virtues. They're a plentiful, year-round source with more protein than most fruit. But they're often thorny, hard to digest, or just plain poisonous. How do leaf-eaters cope?

Sloths and hoatzin birds have complex stomachs, like cows, with bacteria which break down leaves. Food takes days to work through their systems. That's why the hoatzin is called the 'stink bird.'

The howler monkey takes another tack. It deals with toxins in its food by eating a few leaves from a number of different trees.

Leaves don't provide much energy, so leaf-eaters live on the slow track. Sloths and koalas move little, sleeping two-thirds of the time. Howlers space themselves and avoid fights by howling – another energy saver. Many leaf-eaters sunbathe to raise their metabolism.

Not so the capybara, pictured above. This Lab-sized rodent often keeps to the water to avoid getting sunburnt.

QUESTIONS & ANSWERS ABOUT RAINFORESTS
Some of the most-asked questions about tropical rainforests are answered here.

Q **What causes the most damage to tropical rainforests?**

Many things combined. Cutting trees to be sold as timber. Cutting or burning to clear land for cattle or crops. Over-population. Oil drilling and mining pollutes land and water. In this highly interconnected ecosystem, damage to one part damages many.

Q **Don't countries with tropical rainforests need to sell timber, beef, and oil to support their economy?**

These products bring in needed funds. Once sold, however, they can't be replaced. Sustainable products – those that replenish themselves – help the economy and preserve the rainforest. The Philippine island of Palawan discovered a logging ban would save more than $11 million over 10 years. Instead of the one-time price from timber, they can earn continuously from fisheries, tourism, and harvesting products.

Q **How can I avoid eating hamburgers made from cattle grazed on cleared rainforest lands?**

Ask the merchant where the beef came from. For the long term, write Congress for a law to label point of origin. For every four-ounce hamburger from rainforest cattle, about 55 square feet of forest is destroyed. That's one large tree, 50 small ones (20 to 30 species), thousands of insects, and uncounted microorganisms.

Q When I buy products made from wood, how do I know if it's harmful or helpful to the rainforest?

Look, or ask, for a seal with the words "Smart Wood." Rainforest Alliance works with logging companies to manage forests with good social, ecological, and economic results. Woods like mahogany, ebony, teak, rosewood, and koa made into furniture and musical instruments are eligible for seals. Wood cabinets, plywood, veneers, and pencils are harder to trace. Ask the seller.

Q How does ecotourism help preserve tropical rainforests?

Ecotourists visit animal and plant life in nature reserves, encouraging countries to set aside parklands. Visitors spend money for local services and create jobs for park rangers and tour operators. Ecotourism needs your dollars. Participate!

Q What products can I buy that come from renewable rainforest plants?

Many foods: bananas, coffee, sugar, chocolate, vanilla, cashews, paprika, cinnamon, lemons, pineapples. Items made from rattan, jute, and bamboo. Products using latex from rubber trees: tires, tennis shoes, carnauba wax for lipstick, carbon paper, polishes. Items using oils from palm and other trees: perfume, soap, shampoo. Paint and varnish from copa tree resins.

Q Which medicines are made with rainforest plant extracts?

Those used to treat asthma, cancer, malaria, glaucoma, diarrhea, schizophrenic convulsions, and more. Also tranquilizers, painkillers, oral contraceptives, and antibiotics. Only one percent of rainforest plants have been tested for medical uses. Hundreds of cures may yet be discovered.

Q What is the outlook for tropical rainforests – can they be saved?

Many countries have reserves and are trying to create more. Brazil is working to reduce subsidies for cattle ranchers, set aside reserves for indigenous people, and control deliberate forest fires. Nicaragua, Papua New Guinea, and the Philippines no longer export hardwood logs. New farming techniques and harvest of sustainable products helps. Still, everyday 100 acres of rainforest are destroyed, and with them 48 species of plants and animals.

Q What can one person or family do to help save tropical rainforests?

Many things! Conserve water and energy in your home. Recycle newspapers, plastics, and other materials. Carpool, use public transit, walk, or ride a bicycle. Research the origin of items you buy. Join a group working to save rainforests. Write U.S. politicians to set an example by preserving both tropical forests and old-growth forests within the U.S. Tell your friends about the plight of rainforests and how they can help too.

ABOUT THE AUTHOR

Jean Hamilton is a science writer and sometime poet. She lives in her Winnebago – here and there as the spirit moves her – with her cats, Lewis and Clark.

ABOUT THE PHOTOGRAPHERS

Frank Balthis: page 5 lower photo
Hans and Judy Beste/Animals Animals: page 24
John Cancalosi/DRK Photo: page 33 upper photo, 46
John Chellman/Animals Animals: back cover
Earth Scenes/Oxford Scientific Films: page 25 lower photo
E.R. Degginger/Animals Animals: page 16 upper photo
Michael Fogden/DRK Photo: pages 1, 2-3, 10-11, 20-21, 26-27, 40; Animals Animals: page 30 middle photo
François Gohier: pages 6-7, 13
Steven Holt/VIREO: page 2 inset, 18 inset
Breck P. Kent/Animals Animals: page 9 inset
Frans Lanting/Minden Pictures: front cover, page 5 upper photo, 12, 31, 34-35, 36
Richard K. LaVal/Animals Animals: pages 14-15
Wayne Lynch/DRK Photo: page 17
Kevin Schafer and Martha Hill: pages i, 16 lower photo, 22-23, 29, 32, 37, 38, 39
Dr. Nigel Smith/Animals Animals: page 33 lower photo
Larry Ulrich/DRK Photo: page ii
Doug Wechsler/VIREO: pages 4, 18-19, 25 upper photo, 30 upper and lower photos
Belinda Wright/DRK Photo: page 9

SPECIAL THANKS

Linda Countryman, Docent for the Greater Los Angeles Zoo Association, and **Janet Posen**, Science Resource Teacher for San Diego City Schools.

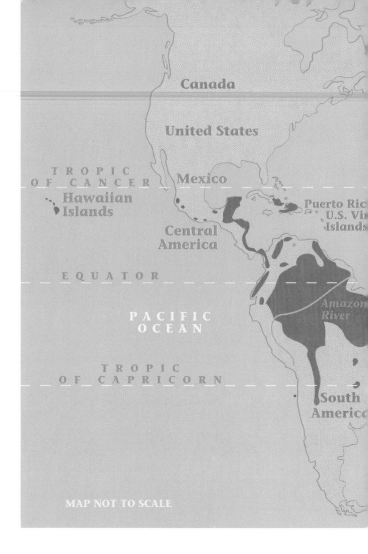

MAP NOT TO SCALE

WHERE TO SEE RAINFORESTS

Many zoos now present rainforest habitats so you can see a sampling of the creatures found there. Visiting actual rainforests is also getting easier. Money generated from ecotourism is a good way to encourage countries to preserve rainforests instead of cutting them.

A partial list:

Latin & South America: Brazil, Costa Rica, Belize, Mexico, Ecuador, Peru, Bolivia, Colombia, Panama

Asia: Indonesia, Philippines, Malaysia, Papua New Guinea, Thailand, India

Africa: Ivory Coast, Ghana, Nigeria, Madagascar, Congo, Zaire

Within the U.S.: National Parks and wildlife refuges in Hawaii, American Samoa, Puerto Rico, and the U.S. Virgin Islands

South Pacific & Australia: Melanesia, Solomon Islands, and Queensland, Australia

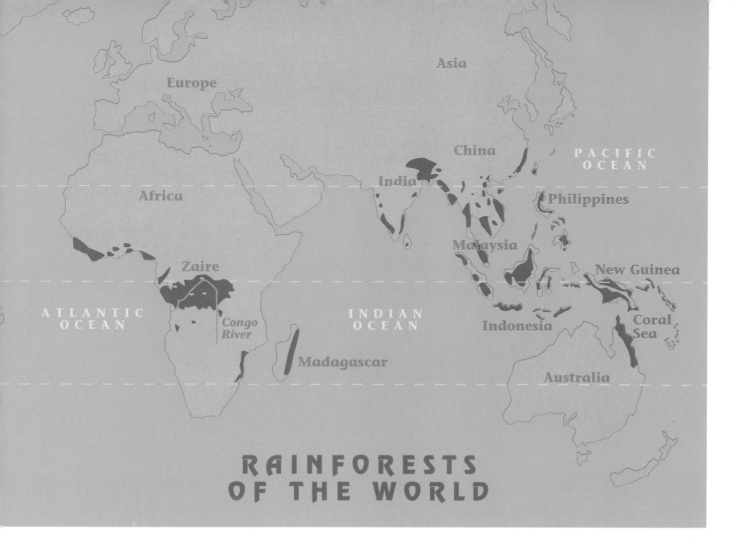

**RAINFORESTS
OF THE WORLD**

TO LEARN MORE

African Wildlife Foundation,
1717 Massachusetts Ave. NW, Suite 602,
Washington, DC 20036; (202) 265-8393
Conservation International, 1015 18th St.
NW, Suite 1000, Washington, DC 20036;
(202) 429-5660
The Nature Conservancy, 1815 N. Lynn St.,
Arlington, VA 22209; (800) 628-6860.
Has "Adopt-an-Acre" program.
Rainforest Action Network, 450 Sansome,
Suite 700, San Francisco, CA 94111;
(415) 398-4404
Rainforest Alliance, 65 Bleecher St.,
New York, NY 10012; (212) 677-1900
Probe International, 225 Brunswick Ave.,
Toronto, Ontario M5S 2M6, Canada;
(416) 964-9223
World Rainforest Movement, 87
Contonment Road, 10250 Penang, Malaysia

BOOKS
✔ *In the Rainforest,* Catherine Caufield
(U. of Chicago Press, 1986)
✔ *Lessons of the Rainforest,* Head &
Heinzman (Sierra Club Books, 1990)
✔ *Life Above the Jungle Floor,* Donald Perry
(Simon & Schuster, 1988)
✔ *The Rainforest Book,* Scott Lewis (Living
Planet Press, 1990)
✔ *Rainforests: A Celebration,* Living Earth
Foundation (Chronicle Books, 1992)
✔ *Tropical Rainforests,* Arnold Newman
(Facts on File, 1990)

FILMS
✔ *Rainforests: Proving Their Worth* (Video
Project, 1990, 30 min.)
✔ *Rain Forest Voices* (New Era Media, 1990)
✔ *Tropical Rainforest* (Media Guild, 1988)

EDUCATIONAL SOFTWARE
✔ *Wings for Learning,* 101 Castleton St.,
Pleasantville, NY 10570; (800) 321-7511

CLOSE-UP
A Focus on Nature

Here's what teachers, parents, kids, and nature lovers of all ages say about this series:

• • • • • • • •

"High-interest topics, written in grownup language yet clear enough for kids..."

"Dazzling, detailed photos. Your beautiful books have a strong educational component—keep it up!"

"Packed with facts and priced right for busy adults."

"Extremely useful for students with reading difficulties..."

"Your book is the best souvenir we could have of our whale-watching trip."

"These books are great gift items for all the bird-watchers, divers, and wildlife artists on my list!"

Silver Burdett Press books are widely available at bookstores and gift outlets at museums, zoos, and aquaria throughout the U.S. and abroad. Educators and individuals wishing to order may also do so by writing directly to:

SILVER BURDETT PRESS
299 JEFFERSON ROAD,
PARSIPPANY, NJ 07054

◆ HABITATS ◆

◆ ANIMALS ◆ BIG & SMALL

◆ BIRDS ◆ IN THE WILD

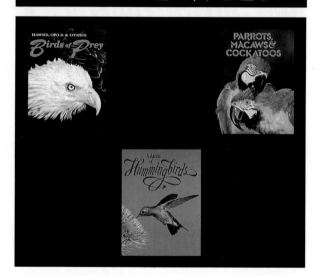

◆ MARINE LIFE ◆

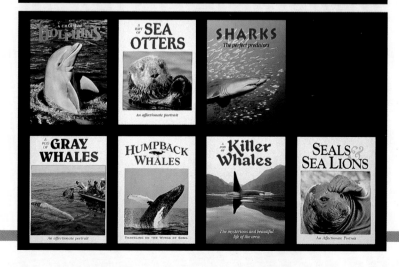

An
Eden
we can
save